The Healing You Can Do

Written by Meghan T. Hindi
Illustrated by Katie m. Berggren

Meghan T. Hindi

Meghan is a wife, mama, animal rescuer and birth advocate living with her family in the mountains of SW Washington State. After giving birth to her second daughter, Adira, she started the YouTube channel Birth Warrior, featuring affirmations, interviews and birth videos to educate and empower. Birth Warrior's following consists mostly of trauma survivors seeking healing. Due to enthusiastic outreach, Meghan felt called to write a book about her survival, healing and transformation. The Healing You Can Do is that story. Written for all ages, this debut book comes from her personal experience and journey to deep healing.
To learn more visit www.TheHealingYouCanDo.com

Katie m. Berggren

Katie has been cited as the #1 Motherhood Artist in America, and her paintings and prints hang in homes in over 70 countries. With her art, Katie seeks to capture moments of peace and wholeness, a sense of love, warmth and connection. Katie lives in Washington State with her husband and two sons, cherishing family moments and creative time.
To learn more visit www.KmBerggren.com

Text Copyright © 2019 by Meghan T. Hindi ~ Illustrations Copyright © 2019 by Katie m. Berggren
All rights reserved. No part of this publication may be reproduced, stored or transmitted in any form without permission in writing from the author. Request for permission to make copies of any part of this work should be directed to Meghan.Hindi@gmail.com.

ISBN 978-1-7330017-0-0 ~ Book design and layout by Katie m. Berggren and Meghan T. Hindi.
Edited by Margo Mejia. Printed and bound in Canada.

Dedicated to survivors of trauma everywhere:
You are a miracle, and you can make it through.
The Healing You Can Do was written for YOU.

To my many children, human and animal ~ you taught me how to love,
how to forgive, and how to embrace my own strength
to move beyond the pain of my past.
I love you more than you could ever know.

To my husband Michael, thank you for believing in me
and standing by me through the dark times
that led to this amazing life we have now.
I love you so much.

To Katie, Margo, and everyone who was brave enough
to tell me their story. You made a difference in my life,
and the lives of others, through this book.
Thank you!
~ M. T. H.

When you were born, little one,
I sang, clapped and cheered!

Because, beautiful child,
You were finally here!

You were so bright and lovely,
So packed full of charm.

My overwhelming love for you
       Could barely fit in my arms.

You have always been more precious
Than you could ever know.

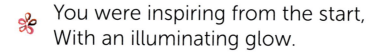 You were inspiring from the start,
With an illuminating glow.

As you grew, day by day,
I admired you from afar.

With such love and awe for you,
And the miracle that you are.

You are a work of art!
So strong, smart and bold!

    I have always been so proud of you.

        You are a wonder to behold!

But as life moved around you,
Other people did, too.

We can't always choose what happens to us,
Nor when, why or by who...

One day, your entire life changed.
You learned a very hard thing.

You were taught that someone can hurt you.

Now you see, there can be pain.

No matter how you were wounded,
The pain can strike so deep.

It can feel like you don't know
Whether to cry, eat or sleep.

But please don't let it dim
The light that is within you.

Don't allow it to darken
All the good things you can do!

You're tougher than anything.
It's just another wall to break through!

        It's not your fault

            They were broken.

        It's not your fault

            That they hurt you.

You are so wildly perfect,
Inside and out.

I know you can't always see it,
But I simply have no doubt!

Please believe you are perfect,
I'll say it again!
My precious child, you have always been.

    You have not been ruined,
        You are not what they say.

    You are priceless, my joy!
        You are more incredible, every day.

Sometimes you may wonder
Where you went in that moment.

Why you cannot remember…
Why your memory is broken.

When I saw danger coming
I pulled you close to me
So you could remain safe,
      Cherished, wild and free.

Only part of you could join me,
      But my dear, it's alright…

      Your beautiful spirit was with me,
            Protected and snuggled up tight.

As you grow beyond that moment,
As you work to let it go...

Please, take care of yourself.
Remember, take it slow.

I know sometimes you feel alone,
Like no one understands.

      Something was stolen, taken from you.
          Now you sit
              with your heart
                  in your hands.

But my child, please know:
I'm always here with you.

Restoring your heart, day by day,
So you can light up the world!

You are inspiring and remarkable!
So deeply worthy of love.

The injustice you've been through,
You can now rise far above!

You are stronger than this!
You can make it through!

        But please know...
                This pain started long before you.

It goes back so much further
Than you could ever know.

Everyone who has hurt you,
Has a deep wound of their own.

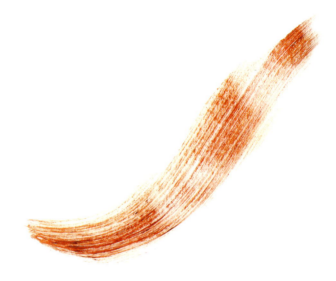

They too were born and grew.
They were just like you.

Then they trusted someone
Who was not kind, gentle or true.

Their trust was broken.
Their safety was stolen.
Then that heartbreak spread on and on.

One way to end this cycle of shame,
Is a brave, bold and honest act...

Fearlessly face the darkness head on,

So you can halt it in its tracks.

One thing I learned in my journey to survive,
That helped me to grow, heal and thrive:
I discovered there is brokenness,
Under every harmful act.

They were lost and aching, and then hurt you,
Because they too were once attacked.

This doesn't make it right, but I promise, it is true.

However, my dear, please remember:
    Empathy can heal, revive and renew!

There is peace in our shared brokenness,
    And wisdom to see we're all the same.

When we acknowledge the pain in everyone,
We have the power to free each other from shame.

Now you, my angel, can fly far beyond this!

With the wisdom you've found,
And the wings that you've built!

Our strongest feathers
        Are words or actions that once hurt.

Each painful moment
Can make you more resilient than before.

        You are unbreakable!
        You will find YOUR way!

        You'll feel the anger and sadness
                            falling
                                away.

You're amazing, you've survived,
You've come so very far!

Though, at times you may still struggle
To see the miracle that you are.

I know it can be hard
     To see the reason for why you're here,

But you have the determination
      To face your future without fear.

You have an incredible chance
To make a difference in this world.

     To spread truth and love to all,
     And see this darkness be unfurled.

You have tremendous purpose,
So many wonderful gifts in you.

Your body may have been hurt,
      Your heart and spirit, too.

But you are truly remarkable!
Look at all that you can do!

      You are not at all defined
           By what has happened to you.

As you grow and build a beautiful life
That is far from where you've been,
You'll be free to find yourself and discover
Who you truly are, deep within.

You will have so many chances,
To see what you're really made of.

You are a formidable force, and yet,
You are capable of so much love.

    You'll find your voice to tell your story,

        Then that story may save lives.

            It will ignite a fire in others,

                It can open up their eyes!

One day you will realize
That the hurt is far behind you.

But please don't forget:
There are still others who will need you
To use what you've learned
To change THEIR world for good.

And if you love them first,
      Think of all that THEY could do!

      So speak out, reach out,
      Never stop encouraging them.

      Work hard to heal the world,
      And to challenge the system.

      Use your wisdom to influence.
            Set the people around you free!

      Then bravely raise your fist in the air
            And ask, "Who else is with me?!"

You were always meant to be here,
You were born for a great reason!

    You are here to live a big life,
        And that is not always easy.

My extraordinary child, I know this to be true:
Your inner light can mend, inspire and renew.

Your empowered compassion is the key to everything.
You cannot fathom all of the joy that you can bring.

Just keep my promise in mind:
Remember all the healing you can do.
    For yourself, those you love,
        And the entire world, too.

All because that hurting someone
                hurt you.

You are a priceless miracle, amazing and so strong.
You have the power to change the world, little one!

The Story Behind This Book

"You take broken things and make them whole..." my friend Naomi said as she gazed in awe of this place. As I told her stories of the animals saved, babies birthed and heartbreaks mended in the past 4 years, she took it all in and seemed deeply moved.

I am no stranger to trauma, and have spent the last 34 years learning to embrace who I really am, despite what I was told by the world.

I first experienced physical, emotional and verbal abuse at the hands of my mother, from my earliest memory. I am genuinely grateful for all of the years of pain, for without it, I would never have become who I am today, and *The Healing You Can Do* would not exist.

My strength was truly tested when I received news that she was diagnosed with ALS and would only live two more years. My sister and I loved and cared for our mother as her body faded. The grief of this season was severe, but to learn empathy through loving and caring for the woman who had hurt me was profoundly healing and deeply transformative.

My mother passed away on May 27, 2014, the day after my 2nd wedding anniversary. I broke away from my extended family at the same time. The amount of loss in that year was utterly heartbreaking. I didn't know it then, but it was also the best thing that could have happened to me.

Something incredible happens when we lose everything: we find the bravery to discover what is right for who we truly are.

In the years that followed, I would have many defining experiences, but none as powerful as the home births of my two daughters. My birth experiences truly changed my life, and how I viewed myself. I could finally release my victim mentality, and accept the love and growth I was capable of. I immediately began speaking out as a birth advocate: encouraging women to embrace their natural power and wisdom in order to heal from their own trauma.

Through my home births, animal rescue, EMDR therapy and introspection, I found empathy for everyone who had hurt me. I saw the shared humanity in all of us, and the pain that they also experienced that caused them to sink to such a low place. Human equality and compassion for all creatures led to more profound personal growth than I ever thought possible.

In June 2018, I felt inspired to write a story for the inner child I had lost long ago, and how I found her again. Throughout creating this book, I have learned so much about myself, other survivors, and the great power that is within us all.

The Healing You Can Do is now my love letter to you, the reader. Whether you have survived trauma, sexual, physical, verbal, emotional abuse or any other event that left you to question your inherent value, please know that you are not defined by those experiences. I see how beautiful you are inside, not despite your trauma, but because of it.

From this day forward, let us begin to tell our stories, listen to one another, and work together to transform the dialogue around trauma and pain. We will see anger released, spirits mended, and lives saved. The world is ready for a change. ~ *M. T. H.*

Read Meghan's full story at **www.TheHealingYouCanDo.com**

Photo Credits: Aleah Stein Photography and Blooming Lotus Photography